BECAUSE,
I
WANT
YOU
TO
KNOW
JUST
HOW
MUCH
I
LOVE
YOU

By Janet L. Cronin

BECAUSE, I WANT YOU TO KNOW JUST HOW MUCH I LOVE YOU

by

Janet L. Cronin

authorHOUSE™

1663 LIBERTY DRIVE, SUITE 200
BLOOMINGTON, INDIANA 47403
(800) 839-8640
WWW.AUTHORHOUSE.COM

First published by AuthorHouse 06/20/05

ISBN: 1-4208-4317-6 (sc)

Printed in the United States of America
Bloomington, Indiana

This book is printed on acid-free paper.

Thank you and congratulations on your purchase of **"BECAUSE, I WANT YOU TO KNOW JUST HOW MUCH I LOVE YOU."** I encourage you to talk to your loved ones and fill in the blanks.

Often times your family members will talk to friends more openly than to family.

Anyone who has a friend or loved one that is leaving on an extended trip. Or do you know someone who is terminally ill? Or maybe an older person you'd just like to get to know better?

My father expired without me being there. Oh how I would have loved to have his feelings written down.

I encourage you to use my book, give it as a gift to those you love. Let's share those feelings today. Tomorrow may be too late, as it was in my case.

Do it for yourself, your friends and your loved ones.

BECAUSE, I WANT YOU TO KNOW JUST HOW MUCH I LOVE YOU is a simple to follow book of questions you may or may not know the answers to. I didn't know all the answers to my father's life. That is in part, why I wrote this book.

Talk to whoever you want this book to be about. Fill in the blanks accordingly. Everyone needs and wants to know the answers.

All too often loved ones, friends and family pass without our simple questions being answered. This book will answer some of the many questions we often forget to ask. Don't let that be you!

Use this book, make it your own, do it for yourself, for your family and for your loved ones. They'll thank you for caring and loving them so.

Most of all it's for the one who you make this book about. The greatest gift of all is being able to help others say what they are unable to put into words. Those words are all too often forgotten.

Let's all use this book. Make it your own so no one will ever forget, your life, thoughts, opinions, wants and wishes. The simple things we all too often forget to ask about.

I encourage you to make this book your own, fill in the blanks and give it to someone you love.

Or better yet, are you friends with some one who has an ill or elderly friend or family member? Maybe you know a young adult who is going to college. Is someone you know going off to serve our country? Phone, fax or e-mail that person and fill in the blanks. Better yet go visit that person and fill in the blanks. Then give this book as a gift or keep it for yourself.

Let's not let anyone's life be forgotten. Especially yours!

Janet L. Cronin

MY

Wants, wishes, woes, worries, thoughts, concerns, feelings, life, emotions, time spent, family, friends, children, children's friends, pets, problems, solutions, favorites, likes, dislikes, habits, personalities, hobbies, jobs, good days, bad days, most embarrassing moments, fears, joys, head, eyes, nose, mouth, hair, face, fingers, arms, legs, ears, elbows, shoulders, knees, fingernails, feet, mind, body, soul, day's spent, nights spent, yesterday's, today's, tomorrow's, successes, failures, secrets, and **HEART** all belong to **YOU.**

Signed _____

Dated _____

PLACE PHOTO HERE

Hello, my name is

_____

I was born on

_____

To _____

And _____

In _____

My nationality is believed to be_____
coming from _____
_____ decent.

I am ____Feet ____inches tall.

I have _____hair and _____eyes.

I weigh _____pounds.

I have _____ tattoos located on my

_____ of _____

_____

I have _____ piercing located on my

_____, _____, and _____

_____

I have broken_____bones.

When _____

Where _____

I have been hospitalized _____ times

for _____

When _____

Where _____

_____

I have _____implants.

I have had my _____
amputated on _____because I

_____

I had to have _____ plates and or pins put
in my _____ because I

_____

I have had or have been in _____
car accidents.

When _____

Where _____

_____

I grew up in_____

_____

As a child I remember my first real
birthday party at

_____

_____

As a child my favorite toys were

_____

_____

I remember having _____
for pets, their names were_____

_____

My grandparents were

My mother's mother

_____

My mother's father

_____

My father's mother

_____

My father's father

_____

I have_____ brothers.

Their names and birthdates are

_____

_____

_____

I have _____ sisters.

Their names and birthdates are

_____

_____

_____

I have _____ step sisters and _____ step brothers.

Their names and birthdates are

_____

_____

_____

I have _____ half sisters and _____ half brothers.

Their names and birthdates are

_____

_____

_____

My very special friends are_____

_____

because _____

_____

My favorite color is

_____

My favorite breakfast is

_____

Lunch is

_____

Dinner is_____

Dessert is_____

Candy is_____

My favorite flower is

_____

My favorite sport is

_____

I went to grade school at

_____

I went to high school at

_____

I went to college at

_____

_____

_____

I Went to trade school at

_____

I went into the Military on

_____

I served in the _____

I was stationed at

_____

I was discharged from the military

_____

I was married on_____
to _____

We honeymooned at

_____

We met/our first date was

_____

We have_____Children
Their names and birthdates are

_____

_____

_____

I divorced _____
On _____

I remarried _____

On _____

We have _____ biological children and
_____ children together.

Their names and birthdates are

_____

_____

_____

_____

My favorite vehicle was the

_____

The worst vehicle was the

_____

My favorite home was

_____

My favorite songs are

_____

_____

As a child/adult I did/didn't play an instrument. It was the

_____

As a child/adult I took _____
lessons.

As a child my best day of grade school was when

_____

_____

As a child my worst day of grade school was when

_____

_____

As a teen my best day of high school was when

_____

_____

_____

As a teen my worst day of high school was when

_____

_____

My favorite teacher was

_____

because _____

_____

My_____ taught me to drive a car. The first car I drove was a

_____

I drove it to the

_____

and _____

_____

_____

After having children the most valuable lesson I learned from my children was

_____

_____

_____

_____

My favorite meal to cook my family is

_____

because _____

_____

My favorite holiday is

_____

because _____

When my children were small my favorite thing to do was

_____

_____

When my children were teens my favorite thing to do was

_____

_____

After my children left home my favorite thing to do is

_____

_____

After my children grew up my worst fear is that

_____

_____

_____

_____

_____

_____

After raising my children I have learned

_____

_____

_____

_____

_____

_____

If I could do it all over again and change anything in my life it would be

_____

_____

_____

_____

_____

_____

When I was about ten years old I really wanted_____

_____

When I first began high school all I really wanted was to

_____

My first real date was with

_____

_____

_____

_____

My first real boy/girl friend was

_____

Do you remember your first kiss?

_____

It was with

_____

My hobbies are

_____

In my spare time I enjoy

_____

_____

After having my first child we/I lived at
and I worked/didn't work at the

_____

_____

_____

_____

_____

_____

_____

_____

After having my 2nd child we/I lived at and I worked/didn't work at

_____

_____

_____

3rd child _____
4th child _____
5th child _____

My biggest accomplishment in my life is that I _____

_____

_____

_____

Given the time to read I enjoy reading

_____

_____

My favorite television show is

_____

If I had to choose a hero it would be

_____

because_____

My favorite vacation had to have been
when we/I _____

_____

The happiest day of my life was when

_____

_____

_____

_____

_____

The saddest day of my life was when

_____

_____

_____

_____

I never told you

_____

_____

_____

_____

I only wish I would have

_____

_____

_____

_____

_____

_____

_____ with you when you were small.

I now_____

_____

_____

_____ with you even though you're grown because I don't ever want you to forget just how much I love you, and loved spending time with you.

Remember today is all we have, right here right now! Yesterday is only a memory. Tomorrow is only a vision. Today is all we have. Make everyday memorable.

Everything happens for a reason; we may never know the reason but we must always continue to go forward.

Learn and live life, don't just let life pass you by. Live the day, the moment the second. Share with others, be kind and treat others the way you would want to be treated. Remember what goes around comes around you only get what you give!

A lady over one hundred years old, when asked what the secret to life was? Said, it was ….**BREATHING**….

Remember that, if you're breathing your okay! Give and receive smiles, don't ever forget to return a smile if you receive one.

Oh yeah, hold each others hands, that's important. The time was short when you allowed me to hold your hand. You're never too old to hold Each others hands.

When I was twenty all I wanted to do was

_____

When I was thirty all I wanted to do was

_____

When I was forty all I wanted to do was

_____

When I was fifty all wanted to do was

_____

When I was sixty all I wanted to do was

_____

When I was seventy all I wanted to do was

_____

When I was eighty all I wanted to do was

_____

When I was ninety all I wanted to do was

_____

When I was one hundred plus all I wanted to do was

_____

After a life time of memories I've enjoyed

_____
_____
_____ the most.

Just pretending I'm

_____
_____
_____
_____ makes me happy.

Remembering the good times and the bad times.   This teaches us all what's right and wrong. Sometimes mistakes and accidents happen.

Life is just like a bowl of fruit. Looks can be deceiving, you never really know until you taste it. Decide then and there if that's really what you wanted.   In either case don't be caught with your mouth full of something you don't want.

Having to find a place to spit can be a bit of a challenge in some circumstances. It's always better to throw the apple away and be a little hungry than to eat the apple with a worm in it and get a belly ache.

Some people may say the worm enhances the apple's flavor. Regardless, often times even a ripe apple will leave you with a bad taste in your mouth.

The moral of the story is: You don't have to take what you don't want. Find a place to spit and go on. Maybe the next piece of fruit will be what you really wanted, or maybe it won't. Keep trying.

Don't settle for something you don't want or don't like the taste of. There's plenty of fruit in the fruit bowl. Try them all if you want…live and enjoy life to its fullest.

See the good in people; we all have some good in us. However, don't be too quick to judge others. What you may see may or may not be real.

Give others ample time, for its only then, you will be able to see others for whom he or she really is. Everyone given enough time will reveal their good and bad sides.

Real people tend to have more good in them than bad, you're the judge, you decide.

Choose your friends wisely, in a crowd they often reflect the kind of person you are.

Jealousy is a wasted emotion, along with worry. Throw those two emotions out of your mind, no one needs them. Find time for yourself and enjoy who you are. You must make yourself happy. No one or nothing, in this world can make you happy except you.

You control your life, stay in control. No one else can do this but you. Don't ever allow someone else to control you or your life. No one but you knows what's right and what's wrong for you.

Your mind, your body, your life should always stay in your control. Only you know for certain what you need and what you're capable of doing. No one can help you until you're willing to help yourself.

Be proud of yourself, I know I am.

Should you ever feel scared, mad or glad? Sometimes, uncomfortable, not knowing why, wanting and needing to hold a hand, I have an idea. Hold mine. I love you and always will. (Trace your hand on the next page).

Just like everything this book has a beginning, middle and an end. In closing I only want you my family, friends and loved ones to know these little secrets, I have shared with you.

Remember they are our secrets. And that I am in no way responsible for stretching the truth, if any of you disagree with my answers and thoughts you'll just have to tell me later.

Catch me if you can. I'm going to be where ever you are. Watching the wind blow or raining on your parade, if you're doing something you shouldn't. Watching you shine on your best days, I'll be smiling. Sometimes I will bring clouds your way as well.

Life isn't easy and often it isn't fun, it's full of patience, hard work, blood sweat and tears. Often time's prayers may help. If you strive to move forward and don't give up, you'll do fine. Don't sweat the little stuff.

Its okay to cry, we cry for many reasons, its okay. Let the clouds rolls by.

The sun will soon shine upon you. Be the best you can possibly be at everything you do. If you fail, go on. Learn from the past and try again.

Oh yeah, should any of the questions be unanswered? Please understand often times the past is better forgotten. Sometimes we just simply can't remember. Or choose to forget.

I have left notes in the blanks so you can ask others for the answers. Maybe someone else will remember. In any case it's worth a shot.

Remember baby, I'll always be there with you. Where ever you are and whatever you're doing, you'll always have all my love. I'll be watching you always. Make me proud. I know you will.

Love,

P.S. Always remember how beautiful you are to me.

NOTES

About The Author

My name is Janet L. Cronin; I was born to Wathen McLean James Jr. and Inez Ruth Wharton on December 16, 1955. I grew up in a suburb of San Francisco.

I have had my share of life's challenges. I was born with a lazy eye and while I was very young had to have my front tooth capped. My parents divorced when I was nine years old, from that time on I rarely saw my father, nor did I see my mother as she was working most of the time.

My education went unnoticed by everyone including myself barely getting by. At sixteen I found a job at McDonald's. Working four hours a day and going to high school four hours a day. I don't know how I managed to acquire enough credits to graduate early in January but I somehow did.

My steady high school boyfriend soon lost my interests regardless of all the forever plans we had made over a three year period. Fast cars, older men caught my attention. With no real family ties, did I mention I was never associated with either set of grandparents.

I found an abusive relationship for a year or so which I was certain it was love and it would last forever. It didn't.

Then I found it my moral obligation to marry someone I felt sorry for. I don't have to tell you what a huge mistake that was.

Then later after I spent some time with myself, working and being self sufficient. Thinking I would never make another mistake. Here came a man that was going to save me with religion. We married for all the wrong reasons. Amazing how one mistake leads to another, there must have been a pattern here don't you think?

I gathered up all of my self worth, found an apartment and continued to work paying my bills and longing for someone who would love me for me. Of course at the time I was unaware of what love meant. Not knowing you must love your-self first before entering into any relation-ship. I had no idea what that meant.

During my parents divorce my mother sent me to the only high school boarding school in the United States. Crane Union High School, in Crane Oregon. It was my freshman year. I only stayed there for one year living in the dormitory and going to school during the week and then going to stay with my uncle and aunt of whom I hardly knew on the weekends.

At the time the adjustment was dif-ficult, never being away from home and being an only child.

Later in my life as an adult I missed the country life and the people I had once met. My seemed to be only happiness was my correspondence with a man who I had gone to high school with in Crane. Keep in mind ten years had passed by.

As an adult tired of the bars, the crowds and the many memories that surrounded me in California where ever I would go would bring to mind an unpleasant memory. I decided to move to Oregon, get a job and see what I could find.

I stayed with my uncle and aunt. After living there a while, I married a rancher who I'd gone to high school with and had been corresponding with well over a year. We have three beautiful children and will soon celebrate our 25th wedding anniversary.

My life is wonderful and I cherish each and every minute of each and everyday. I tell my children if I have the opportunity to see or to speak with you today. Today just may the best day of my life.

I presently work at a hospital as a phlebotomist. The job has taught me a lot about myself and a lot about people. I have been present many times when family, friends and others have expired. I don't know why people touch my heart so but they do.

I want to share my feelings, thoughts and cares with my family so when the time comes that I too will pass they will have something of me to hold on to when I can't be there.

Many people have told me so many things. I know I never could possibly pass them on to the appropriate people. So I have chosen to write this book for you, and for anyone you know and love who would want to share their lives with their loved ones.

So please as difficult as it may be to accept the fact that we are only here for such a short period of time. In time we all will pass. Please fill in the blanks, and make this book your own.

Write things to your loved ones that you've forgotten or are to afraid to say. Do it for your loved ones, do it for yourself. You may never know how much it may help others. In the days ahead, reading your thoughts, your wants and wishes. To have something to hold that shares your life's most memorable and not so memorable memories.

Filling in the blanks in this book will help you express yourself, and your thoughts of those days gone by. Doing this may help the ones you love understand you better. Let no one be without these simple questions being answered. Let no ones life be forgotten.

So in closing I dedicate this book to my father, and to everyone who make this book there own. To my children who probably won't understand what this all means until they grow older. Last of all to my husband, my soul mate, my very best friend. Without you I wouldn't have been me. I love you with all my heart and soul.

Love
Janet L. Cronin